Now and Then

A Play

David Campton

A Samuel French Acting Edition

SAMUEL FRENCH

FOUNDED 1830

SAMUELFRENCH-LONDON.CO.UK
SAMUELFRENCH.COM

ISBN 978-0-573-03367-4

www.samuelfrench-london.co.uk

www.samuelfrench.com

FOR AMATEUR PRODUCTION ENQUIRIES

UNITED KINGDOM AND WORLD EXCLUDING NORTH AMERICA

plays@SamuelFrench-London.co.uk

020 7255 4302/01

Each title is subject to availability from Samuel French,

depending upon country of performance.

CHARACTERS

NOW
Bella
Midge
Guide
Sightseers

THEN
Wise Woman of Wickwell
Servant
Customer

The action takes place in a room in an old house, both now and four hundred years ago

NOW AND THEN

A comfortless room. There are no curtains, hangings or carpets—though the floor may possibly be strewn with rushes. There is little furniture, and that is wooden and hard. Against a table with writing materials is a chair, and a high-backed armchair stands in a commanding position with a stool close to it. There are two doors to the room, facing each other at R *and* L. *The* R *door is open*

A woman enters. This is the Wise Woman of Wickwell, a vigorous person in late middle age, dressed in Tudor style. Behind her she drags a younger woman, who might be a servant

Wise Woman In here, vixen! You'll do my bidding next time, I warrant. Who am I, eh? And what are you? Patch. Blight. Spot.

She swings the Servant towards the stool. The Servant sits, says nothing, but sniffs occasionally. The Wise Woman continues her harangue. She has her say, but cannot bring herself to finish. Every time she reaches a conclusion and pauses for breath, her indignation boils over again. The result is a series of outbursts punctuated by pauses

Since when have you been mistress of this house? Eh? Since when have you been the Wise Woman of Wickwell? Hah? You'll not do this; you'll not do that! You'll do as you're bid. (*She sits in the armchair*)

The Servant has her back to the Wise Woman, and is half-frightened, half-defiant

Sorry for the fool, are you? Providence puts honey in the flowers. Do you grieve because bees help themselves?

Pause

Besides, there's no promise ever made. Where there's no promise, there's no cozening. So when the next fool comes knocking at the door, you'll perform, wench. You'll perform.

A Woman strides through the open door. She is tough, tweedy, and the terror of half-a-dozen committees. Incongruously, though, she is dressed in twentieth-century costume. Her suit is plain, and her only jewellery a brooch like an antique buckle. She marches to the centre of the room, ignoring the Wise Woman and her Servant. She looks around her, grunts, then marches out again

Neither the Wise Woman nor her Servant seem to see her

It's little enough you do, anyway. Who works on the gulls, anyway? Who slips the words into your mouth? You're a nothing, wench. A stuffed owl would serve as well, and eat less.

The twentieth-century Woman returns

Twentieth-century Woman This way, Midge.

A wispy, nervous person trails in after her. She is a little younger than her companion. She, too, wears modern dress

Midge Bella—aren't we trespassing?
Bella We paid. See what there is to see. It cost enough.

They look around the room, but still do not see, and are not seen by the Tudor women

Wise Woman Servants are come by easily enough. Suppose I turn you out. Will your scruples line your belly and cover your back? I can pick up another outcast any day. With more gratitude.
Bella Poor value. I said we should have gone to Windsor.
Wise Woman Ingratitude is a sin. Remember that and mend your ways.
Midge We've *been* to Windsor, Bella.
Bella There's something to see at Windsor.
Midge Twice.
Bella There's always something to see at Windsor.
Wise Woman If I chastise you, it's for your own salvation. I wouldn't have you go to Hell for ingratitude.

Bella smacks the back of the armchair

Bella Look at this.
Wise Woman Be grateful.
Bella Fake.

The Wise Woman stands

Wise Woman Ah. Did you hear? Another goose at the door,
  ready for plucking. (*She turns to the Servant*) And you—you'll
  play as I taught you. Or I'll instruct you with the birch.

The Wise Woman goes out through the still-open door

Bella sits in the armchair

Bella There's nothing to recommend the place.
Midge It's—romantic. (*She moves to the table on the other side
  of Bella from the Servant*)
Servant I don't care. (*She puts out her tongue, then sulks*)
Bella (*turning to the Servant, but not seeing her*) What did you say?
Midge I said—it's romantic.

Bella turns, surprised to see Midge on the other side of her

Bella How did you get over there?
Midge I walked.
Bella You whispered in this ear. How could you do that from
  over there?
Midge I didn't. Look at this inkwell.
Bella It's the acoustics.
Midge I'm sure it's genuine.
Bella Interesting.
Midge Yes.
Bella Say something else.
Midge Solid pewter.
Bella Eh?
Midge (*uncertainly*) Solid—pewter?
Bella That's a daft thing to say. An echo. If it wasn't an echo, it
  was the wind.
Midge Oh! Do you think . . . ?
Bella No. And you don't either. (*She stands up*)
Servant But that birch hurts.
Midge The past lies all around us.

Bella Bricks and stone. Planks and plaster. They're what lie around us. Nothing more.

Midge (*drifting to the stool where the Servant is sitting*) People lived here once.

Bella And died. Were buried, crumbled to dust, and that was that. I heard a draught through a keyhole, and that was that.

The Servant sighs

Midge I didn't hear it.

Bella You're too lost among moonbeams to hear anything. I believe in faulty plumbing and ill-fitting doors. I don't believe in . . . Nor do you. It's only an escape hole. You dream up another world because this isn't good enough for you.

Midge Bella . . .

Bella It's good enough for me.

Midge Please, Bella.

Servant I must obey.

Midge It's only one afternoon.

Bella Wasted.

Midge I only have one birthday a year. On your birthday we went to a wrestling match, but I didn't complain.

Bella I'm not complaining. We're overcharged to gawk at a ruin with a load of junk, but I'm not complaining. The tea was like water, but I'm not complaining. I put up with your mooning . . .

Midge I'm sorry.

Bella I said I'm not complaining.

Servant Wise Woman of Wickwell. She's not so wise.

Midge All right. Let's go home.

Bella Not before I've had my moneysworth. (*She is about to sit on the stool*)

Midge (*warning*) Bella!

Bella (*pausing*) What now?

Midge I don't think we're supposed to use the furniture.

Bella What else is it for? (*She sits in the armchair*)

Servant She's long enough coming up. Happen she's counting her silver. (*She gets up, goes to the open door, and listens*)

Bella We paid enough for it.

The L door opens, and the Guide comes in, accompanied by a

*group of Sightseers. The Guide is a prim, tight-lipped person,
accustomed to reeling off information*

Guide And here we have one of the oldest . . . (*She stops on
seeing the enthroned Bella*)

The Sightseers twitter among themselves

Visitors should have remained with the party.
Bella Why? What have we missed?
Guide And that chair is not meant for sitting on.
Bella (*getting up*) I knew there was something wrong with it.
Guide This house is furnished exactly as it would have been in
olden times.
Bella (*pretending to examine the chair*) Woolworths. Nineteen-
thirty.
Guide No expense has been spared. This furniture is as genuine
as—as that brooch.
Bella Woolworths. Nineteen-seventy.
Midge Oh!
Guide (*passing over the interruption*) This is the oldest part of the
house. Fifteenth century. This room was old when Queen
Elizabeth slept here. Other parts were added later. The entire
East Wing was built by Sir Exton, who died shortly afterwards.
Bella Who's surprised?
Guide Now, if you will kindly pass out to the left along the
gallery . . . (*She stands by the door*)

The Sightseers move out

The Servant hears someone coming, and hurries back to her stool

Midge and Bella are the last to leave the room

Guide I am waiting.
Bella (*bleating*) Baa! Come on, Midge. Join the sheep.
Midge Bella, you know how much that brooch cost me.

Midge hurries out after Bella

Guide Thank you.

The Guide goes out and shuts the door. Almost immediately the Wise Woman and her Customer come in through the other door. The Customer is expensively dressed in Tudor style. She is rather ill at ease, having lowered herself to visit the Wise Woman. She pauses in the doorway, but is propelled forward by the Wise Woman

Wise Woman Forward, madam. Never block a doorway.
Customer Is it bad luck?
Wise Woman It's bad manners.

The Customer looks around her, a little disappointed by the bareness of the room

Customer Is this the room? But . . .
Wise Woman Where are the black cat, the stuffed lizard, the bubbling cauldron? I respect your intelligence, madam, as I hope you do mine. That creature is all the paraphernalia I need.

The Wise Woman waves to the Servant, who stands

Customer (*slightly alarmed*) Will she remain while . . .?
Wise Woman She is my instrument. Be seated.
Customer (*with an embarrassed giggle*) A foolish errand. (*She sits in the armchair*)
Wise Woman As you will. It's *your* errand.
Customer So many miles, and such a price, to pursue a bauble. A buckle. Merely a lost shoe buckle. But it has sentimental attachments, or I'd never have turned to a fortune teller.

The Servant giggles at this affront to the dignity of the Wise Woman, who snorts

Do you raise the Devil? Oh, I'm not prejudiced against witches.
Wise Woman If your baubles are as loose as your tongue, no wonder you lose 'em. I am the Wise Woman of Wickwell. I have powers—as madam shall perceive. But I abhor magic, I abjure spells, and I have no truck with conjuring.
Customer Indeed? But can you find my trinket without them?
Wise Woman In time.
Customer Time? If I had time, would I pay your monstrous fee? I must have the article.

Wise Woman Before your husband misses it?

The Customer gives a little cry, then composes herself again

Customer Before he finds it. He has a sharp temper and a quick
  blade. Lady, my feet have strayed.
Wise Woman And your shoes on them.
Customer With buckles.
Wise Woman Why not search in the place you fear?
Customer I told you, my feet had strayed.
Wise Woman And strayed?
Customer And strayed! (*She remembers the Servant*) She is—
  discreet?
Wise Woman As a stick.

The Wise Woman beckons to the Servant, who crosses to the table

  I use her as a divining-rod. Sit.

The Servant remains standing

  Still rebellious?
Servant (*to the Customer*) My lady, don't be——
Customer (*interrupting*) She can talk?
Wise Woman No more than necessary. Sit this instant, or you'll
  wish that you *could* sit!
Servant I wouldn't do her bidding, my lady, but she beats me.
Customer No more than necessary, I've no doubt. Ever the way
  with servants—wayward, ungrateful and lazy.
Wise Woman Sit!
Customer Do as you are bid, wench. Time flies and my husband
  prowls. Sit!
Servant Then I'll not be sorry for you. (*She sits by the table*)
Wise Woman What are you muttering?
Servant I'll tell what I see, and no more.
Wise Woman You'll see what I tell you to see. (*She puts the large
  inkwell in front of the Servant*)
Wise Woman Look into that.
Servant Ink. Black ink.
Wise Woman There'll be more anon. (*She strokes the Servant's
  head*)
Wise Woman I work with the elements. There are four elements—
  earth, air, fire and water. I draw the element of air from this

minion, and send it questing. It sees what it sees, and what it sees is reflected in that dark pool. If your property lies above the earth it cannot be hidden.

Customer Then where . . .?

Wise Woman Patience. Of course, if it should be buried or lie under water, then the elements of earth and water must be employed. Being more difficult and dangerous, the experiment commands a higher fee.

Customer Not from me. My husband is neither fish nor mole. If the bauble should be drowned or buried, let it lie.

Wise Woman What see you now?

Servant Ink.

Wise Woman The element is reluctant to be drawn. Madam, where should it rest first?

Customer Work on the element, woman. Not on me. You picture the place, and I'll confirm it.

But the Wise Woman keeps a close watch on the Customer's reactions

Wise Woman A chamber, wench. Do you see a chamber?

Customer A chamber? Aye. A chamber would be a likely place to lose a buckle. (*She smiles*)

Wise Woman A bedchamber.

The Customer's smile disappears

Yes, you see a bedchamber. You see . . .

Servant Black ink.

Wise Woman (*who would like to box the Servant's ears, but the time is not appropriate*) As yet the vision is dark, but it will clear. There is a bed, and on it lie . . .

Customer (*starting*) Who?

Wise Woman Clothes, madam.

The Customer is annoyed at having given something away

Servant (*her speech becoming blurred*) Ink. Black. Black. Black . . .

Wise Woman We progress. Already we have a gentleman's bed-chamber.

Customer You're welcome to it.

Servant I see—I see.

Customer What?

Servant A buckle.
Customer Where?
Servant Here.
Wise Woman There.
Servant 'Tis worn. Not as a buckle, though. But here. Near the heart.
Customer Oh, the villainous rhymester. Would he destroy us both?
Servant This is no man.
Wise Woman A woman?
Servant But I see. I never saw before, but now I have the sight.
Wise Woman This is not what I taught you. Speak the lines, flibbertigibbet. My lines.
Servant She holds her hand to her head. She looks wondrous, amazed.
Wise Woman Confine yourself to facts, wittol. Leave the embroidery to me.
Servant I can draw her.
Wise Woman I'll draw thee. Hang and quarter, too, for your impertinence. (*To the Customer, grandly*) I will interpret.
Servant She comes. Now!

The door L opens, and Bella enters

Bella Somebody call? (*She notices the tableau*) A pageant! Included in the price of admission?

The Servant freezes, eyes wide with fear and wonder

Wise Woman The call has been answered, madam.
Bella You were late getting into place, though. The party went by.
Wise Woman Your silver was well spent.
Bella Oh, I'm on my own, so you needn't keep up the act.
Wise Woman Scan the pool of ink once more.
Bella You need a better wardrobe-mistress.
Wise Woman Search, wench!
Bella These bits of tat are too secondhand.
Wise Woman Look!
Bella Must have seen a hundred productions of *Merrie England*.
Wise Woman Look!

Slowly the Servant turns to face Bella

Servant She came!

Bella I heard you shout.

Wise Woman Bestir yourself.

Customer Is this part of the ceremony?

Servant 'Tis the stranger—dressed as no woman ever dressed before!

Bella I beg your pardon!

Servant Shorn hair. Immodest skirts. Half-man, half-woman.

Bella That's quite enough.

Servant Say you see her.

Customer I see nothing.

Wise Woman The wench is in a playful mood.

Bella Is she?

Servant I did as you bade. What more can I do?

Bella You can stop this nonsense. Now!

Servant She's angry.

Wise Woman She? Dust in the air. No more.

Bella Now you listen to me . . .

Servant Her eyes spark threats.

Wise Woman This is not what you rehearsed, half-wit.

Bella Who's in charge here?

Servant My mistress.

Wise Woman I'm glad you're in mind of it.

Bella (*to the Wise Woman*) You, then. You.

Customer She performs prettily, but I've no time for mummery.

Bella Nor have I. Dressing up is one thing. Making mock of the customers is another.

Servant Speak softly to her, madam.

Wise Woman Waste my breath on your brainstorms?

Bella I'll complain to the management.

Servant Bid her return the trinket.

Bella Impertinence!

Customer Is the creature possessed?

Wise Woman Bread and water in the cellar for a week. That's the treatment.

Servant But, madam. She has the buckle.

Customer An invisible buckle? It's a conspiracy to defraud.

Bella This joke won't be repeated.

Customer Produce my property or return the fee.

Bella I'll write to *The Times*! (*She stamps to the door and opens it*)

Midge enters as Bella opens the door

Servant Saints protect us. Here's another!
Midge There you are, Bella.
Wise Woman Vex me no more.
Bella Did you hear them calling, too?
Servant But there they are!
Midge You shouldn't have left us again.
Servant There! And there!
Midge The Guide dried up completely in the middle of the fourth
  Baron's marriage.
Customer Who is cheating whom?
Bella Shut up!
Midge Bella!
Bella Not you. Them.
Wise Woman I can explain, madam.
Midge Them?
Wise Woman Why should this gosling see what is denied her
  betters?
Customer Why? (*She thinks it over*)
Bella You. What is it in aid of? Charity? Publicity?
Midge Bella, I'm here.
Bella I'm talking to them.
Wise Woman The wench has notions above her station—con-
  versing with beings invisible to us.
Midge Them. (*She thinks it over*)
Servant I tell the truth.
Wise Woman (*in her ear*) What have you to do with the truth?
  (*She leads the Servant back to the table*) Speak as you're ex-
  pected to speak. Neither more nor less. (*To the Customer*) She
  regrets her lapse already.

*The Servant sits at the table again. The Wise Woman stands behind
her*

Bella Back to the performance, eh?
Midge Bella—I'm the one who has headaches.
Wise Woman Give voice.
Midge Who are you talking to?
Bella You can see them, can't you?
Servant I see nothing.

Wise Woman (*threateningly*) Nothing?
Servant Yet.
Bella Midge!

Midge shakes her head

Don't you play the fool. I've had a belly-full of that lot.
Midge You haven't told me what I'm supposed to see.
Bella Whatever's there.
Midge (*understanding at last*) Ah.
Customer Your elements take their time.
Wise Woman When the Wise Woman commands, they obey.
Bella Midge, tell me. Can you see them?
Midge Yes, I see them.
Bella As they would have been four hundred years ago.
Midge So the Guide said.
Bella (*relieved*) Ah!
Midge A table, a chair, and a pewter inkwell.
Bella Not the furnishings, donkey. The people.
Midge The people?
Customer (*yawning pointedly*) Heigh-ho.
Wise Woman Quickly, loon. Bring forth. Something. Anything.
Bella That overdressed strumpet.
Servant Overdressed strumpet?
Customer Who?
Wise Woman Not present company.
Midge Is she under the table?
Bella I don't believe in ghosts.
Servant (*standing and turning*) We're no ghosts.
Wise Woman (*shaking her*) Wanton! (*To the Customer*) Patience,
    madam. (*Forcing the Servant to sit again*) Down, offal!
Bella You. You can see me and hear me.
Servant I see. I hear.
Wise Woman Then speak.
Bella Why the nonsense?
Midge Sit down, dear. I'll try to find a cup of tea and an aspirin.

Midge makes for the door, but is stopped by a cry from Bella

Bella Midge. I'm not imagining anything!
Midge Of course not, Bella. It's my fault if I can't see them.
Bella Rub your eyes. Those lunatics are solid enough. You!

Bella strides towards the Servant, who jumps up with a shriek, pushing the Wise Woman aside

Servant Keep away!
Wise Woman ⎱ Hussey! *(Speaking together)*
Bella ⎰ Fool!

The Servant runs for safety behind the Customer, who shrieks

Customer She's possessed!
Bella Neither of us is wanting.
Midge Of course we're not.
Servant These creatures threaten us.
Customer (*putting the Wise Woman between herself and the Servant*) Your spirits have made away with her wits.
Wise Woman Elements.
Customer Your elements——
Wise Woman (*interrupting*) Know their place.
Bella For the last time . . .
Servant (*facing her*) Whatever you be—element of earth, fire, or water.
Bella I'm as solid as yourself.
Servant Goblin, ghost, or fairy—make yourself known to my mistress before she beats me.
Customer She entreats empty air. Either she pleads with spirits, or she's mad.
Wise Woman There are no spirits.
Servant What are these?
Customer Tie her up and send for the priest. There are devils to be cast out.
Wise Woman Wait. Wait.
Customer At least summon the Constable. If she proves violent . . .
Servant But I'm afraid, too.
Bella Of me?
Servant Of you—and her—and her—and her. And myself.
Bella You frighten yourself?
Midge No, Bella. I'm not frightened. I'm your sister.
Bella I don't believe it.
Midge But I am. I've always been your sister.
Servant If these be none of your doing, ma'am. I have powers.
Bella This truck with spooks belongs to back-parlour charlatans,

not hard-headed committee members.
Customer Is it safe to seize her?
Servant I can raise devils.
Wise Woman Better leave her.
Bella Three Tudor ladies. I'd swear it before any Commissioner for Oaths.
Midge Not you, Bella. I'm the one with fancies.
Bella Midge, I'm frightened.
Servant You—afeard of me?
Midge You mustn't be frightened, Bella. You're the one who locks up at night. You're the one who looks for burglars.
Servants I command devils, and they tremble.
Midge If you're afraid, who's to take care of us?
Customer Play to her humour. What does the devil say?
Wise Woman I do not deal with devils.
Customer You may not, but she . . .

Bella shuts her eyes and puts her hands over her ears

Midge Bella!
Servant Devil, did you hear my lady?
Bella Buzz, buzz, buzz. My head is clear. My feet are firm on the ground.
Midge They always were. Come away.
Servant Answer.
Bella I'm not under your orders.
Midge Of course not, Bella. You never were.
Customer Does the devil reply?
Servant 'Tis an obstinate devil, lady.
Customer But under control.
Servant I'd not care to say. I never raised one afore.
Customer Amateur!
Servant I'll command gently. Devil, sweet devil, my lady seeks your help.
Bella That trollop? They mustn't provoke me. Non-existent creatures. Midge, hold my hand.
Midge There, there. I'm with you.
Servant Where did she lose her buckle?
Bella I neither know nor care.
Midge No, Bella. You never did.

Servant But you have it now, devil—on your bodice, if it is a bodice.

Bella This? (*She touches the brooch*)

Midge It's genuine, Bella. The man in the shop said it was genuine. He said I could take it back if you didn't like it, but you seemed to like it.

Bella What's this to you?

Midge It's very old.

Servant She lost it. In a place where her husband must not find it.

Midge We should have gone to Windsor.

Bella Could this frivol spark over a gap in time?

Customer The devil replied.

Servant 'Tis a very rude devil.

Bella There's only one explanation. When a person sees things that no-one else can . . .

Midge I'm trying, Bella. I'm trying.

Customer I'm waiting.

Midge (*desperately pointing in the wrong direction*) There they are!

Bella No. There!

Midge Go away, things. Go away. Leave my sister alone.

The Servant giggles

Customer Enough of these private jokes with the nether world.

Midge Have they gone?

Bella shakes her head

Oh, Bella. (*She holds her sister's hands comfortingly*)

Customer Give answer, or I'll have you beaten.

Servant Very well, then. The devil says my lady is a trollop, and if justice were done, she'd be whipped from Wickwell to London Bridge. But either her spouse knows of it, or he does not know.

Customer Either the moon is made of green cheese, or it is not. To the point.

Servant If, after so many sports, he has discovered nothing, he is not like to now. But in any case my lady will lie herself out of any extremity.

Customer Enough!

Bella Enough!

Servant Enough?

Bella (*unfastening the brooch*) Here or there. Then or now. Alive of dead.
Customer My property.
Bella Tell her ladyship to collect.
Servant The devil offers it.
Bella (*holding it out*) Will you take it?
Customer Pluck it from the air?
Servant I'll lead you.

The Customer is undecided. She looks at the Wise Woman, who has not yet made up her mind how to deal with this situation. The Servant holds out her hand

Customer You'll answer for any injuries, woman.

The Customer reluctantly takes the Servant's hand, then allows herself to be led towards Bella

Midge Bella . . .
Bella Shush!

The Servant brings the Customer's hand to Bella's hand

Servant There.
Customer There. (*She looks fascinated at Bella's hand, then her glance travels along Bella's arm, and comes to rest on Bella's face*)
Customer There and there and there and there and . . . (*She screams. She backs away from Bella, giving shrieks like blasts on a whistle*) Eee! Eee! Eee! Eee! Eee!
Wise Woman What ails you, madam? There's nothing to harm you. You have my assurance. There are no spirits or demons. The pool of ink is no more than ink. But I am the Wise Woman of Wickwell. If anything is to be unveiled, I unveil it.
Servant (*pointing to Bella*) See you that?

With a final shriek the Customer turns and runs through the door R

Wise Woman Madam. My lady!

The Wise Woman follows the Customer

The Servant goes to the door, then pauses

Servant Devil or spirit. My thanks.

The Servant curtseys, then goes out

Bella hurries to the door after the Servant

The Guide enters, meeting Bella

Bella You!
Midge (*excitedly*) I see her, Bella. I see her, too.
Guide For forty pence you get one conducted tour. You are not entitled to take up residence.
Bella Did you see them? On the stairs.
Guide I led the party out. I came back for you.
Bella Tell me . . .
Guide (*crossing over to the other door*) This way, if you please.
Bella Is this part of the house haunted?
Guide A nun is reputed to walk in the West Wing. If you'd stayed with us you would have learned that.
Bella But—nothing here?
Guide Before renovation this was a store-room. Nothing ever happened here. (*She opens the door*) The exit.
Bella (*looking through the R door*) I thought . . . There . . .
Guide Now!
Midge My sister isn't well. She came in here so as not to upset the others.
Guide Indeed?
Midge If you knew what gratitude was, you'd find a cup of tea instead of barking.

The Servant returns through the R door. She looks around the room, but does not see the party

Bella does not see her

Bella Midge . . .
Midge Don't worry, dear. I'll look after everything. Tea?
Guide This way.

The Guide and Midge go out

Bella We should have gone to Windsor.

Bella goes out and shuts the door

The Servant seats herself in the armchair

After a few seconds the Wise Woman returns

Wise Woman What are you doing in my chair?
Servant (*waving to the stool*) Be seated, woman.
Wise Woman I need no invitation from you, slut.
Servant How she ran! How she screamed for the groom! The
 story will be all over the shire by Friday. I have powers.
Wise Woman You can act, I grant you.
Servant She paid well.
Wise Woman That's none of your concern.
Servant We must agree how to divide the pelf.
Wise Woman Share with a hireling?
Servant Share with the Wise Woman of Wickwell.
Wise Woman I am the Wise Woman of Wickwell.
Servant You? Then what am I? Sit.

The Wise Woman slowly sits on the stool

The Guide opens the door and looks in

Guide Nobody there. Nobody at all.

The Guide goes out, shutting the door, as—

the CURTAIN *falls*

FURNITURE AND PROPERTY LIST

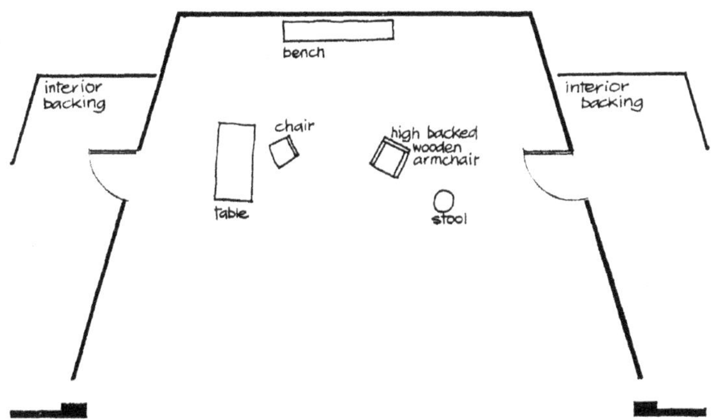

On stage: Table. *On it:* old-fashioned writing materials, including ink-
  well
High-backed wooden armchair
Stool
Small chair
Bench

Personal: **Bella:** antique brooch-like buckle

LIGHTING PLOT

Property fittings required: nil
A room

To open:　General daylight effect, rather subdued and shadowy

No cues